Girls Like You

Girls Like You

MARGOT DOUAIHY

Works produced at Clemson University by the Center for Electronic and Digital Publishing (CEDP), including *The South Carolina Review* and its themed series "Virginia Woolf International," "Ireland in the Arts and Humanities," "James Dickey Revisited," and "African American Literature," may be found at our website: http://www.clemson.edu/cedp. Contact the director at 864-656-5399 for information.

Copyright 2015 by Clemson University
ISBN 978-0-9908958-2-4

Published by Clemson University Press at the Center for Electronic and Digital Publishing, Clemson University, Clemson, South Carolina.

Produced with the Adobe Creative Suite CS6 and Microsoft Word. This book is set in Adobe Garamond Pro and was printed by Ricoh USA.

Editorial Assistants: Karen Stewart, Charis Chapman.

Front cover art and illustrations on pages 1, 15, 29, 41, 45, and 53 by Bri Hermanson.

To order copies, contact the Center for Electronic and Digital Publishing, Strode Tower, Box 340522, Clemson University, Clemson, South Carolina 29634-0522. An order form is available on our website.

Table of Contents

Acknowledgments • vii

❦

I

Maidservant • 2
Girls Like You • 3
Perch • 4
Past Lives • 5
Kimono • 6
Four Ways to View a Fist of Clay • 7
Fog • 8
Festival of the Hungry Ghost, Hong Kong • 9
At Saint Vincent's Hospital Watching My Girlfriend
Get Her Stomach Pumped • 10
Endings • 11
Rorschach • 12
Wife • 13
Avon • 14

II

New York • 16
Heart • 17
Mother's Day • 18
First Time • 19
Venice • 20
How To View a Solar Eclipse • 21
Globe • 22
Too Late • 23
Ten-Word Love Stories • 24
End of the Holiday • 25
Rock • 26
Scarlet Fever • 27
Envy • 28

III

I Said the Bruises Were From Dancing • 30
Confession • 31
Plum • 32
Reality Show • 33
Neither • 34
Text Me • 35
Survival Instinct • 36
How We Do It • 37
Start • 38
Tiny Sun • 39
Oracle • 40

IV

Reminder • 42
Who Killed Belle Starr? • 43
Wax • 46
Gimme a Break • 47
V • 48
Tag • 49
Shore • 50
Fourteen Ways • 51
I Want to Be Your Jukebox • 52

V

Who's the Boss? • 54
Thelma & Louise, Deleted Scene • 55
Don't Worry • 56
Gold • 57
Jasmine • 58
Water • 59
Shorts • 60
My Money • 61
Game Over • 62
Modern Women • 63

***A Note on the Poet* • 64**

Acknowledgments

"Maidservant," "Past Lives," and "Perch" appeared in *The Sow's Ear Review*.
"Ten-Word Love Stories" and "Too Late" appeared in *The Madison Review*.
"Wife" appeared in *The Moth Magazine*.
"Water" appeared in the *Catamaran Literary Reader*.
"My Money" appeared in *The New Guard Review*.
"Who Killed Belle Starr?" appeared in the *Belle Rêve Literary Journal: Editor's Choice*.
"Oracle" appeared in *Big Bridge*.
"Rock," "Shorts," and "Festival of the Hungry Ghost, Hong Kong" appeared in *Ducts*.
"Tiny Sun" appeared in *The Common*.
"Who's the Boss?" appeared in *Philadelphia Stories*.
"Text Me" appeared in *Stress Fractures: Essays on Poetry* (Tom Chivers, ed., Penned In The Margins Press, 2010).
Many of these poems appeared in my chapbook, *I Would Ruby If I Could* (Factory Hollow Press, 2013), some in slightly altered forms.

Sincere gratitude to my readers, publishers, and supporters: Factory Hollow Press, Robin Vaughan-Williams, Anne Marie Fyfe, Jack Underwood, and the F. Lammot Belin Arts Foundation. Thank you to Clemson University Press: Wayne Chapman, a champion of poetry; John Morgenstern, managing editor extraordinaire; and the talented Clemson University Press art team.

Gratitude for the wisdom and guidance of Maura Dooley, Lynn Emanuel, Ed Ochester, and Greta Stoddart. Thanks especially to Jan Beatty whose poetry shakes the very foundation; your work inspires me to take risks and push further.

Effusive gratitude to Bill Black, Tonya Hegamin, Amy Lemmon, and Lucy Powell: your quick insight, encouragement, and own dexterous writing dare me to mine deeper. I am lucky to know you. Thanks to Emily Bludworth de Barrios—your confidence in my poetry has been a stable life raft in choppy waters.

Special thanks to Puya Abolfathi, Amoreen Armetta, Miriam Belblidia, Pearl Bell, Kim Black, Mia Black, Claire Cox, Marc Evans, Nicole DiDio Johnson, Ryan Green, Margo Fotta, Leah Foster, Stacy Giovannucci, Jennifer Huxta, Brent Korson, Erin Manns, Lina Mounzer, Kirsten Nelson, Brian Newman, Nora Romanoff, and Tai Power Seeff. You have listened to my crazy ideas, read my inscrutable scraps, spun the globe, and stood in the rain with me. Eternal gratitude to Rebecca Ferris for your unfailing ability to recite Morrissey lyrics, our E.E.

Cummings trip, and decades of friendship and high jinks. Thanks to my yoga community for the loving kindness.

To the unicorns, Anthony Psaila and Tonya Hegamin: from London to Florence and all points in between, you have offered literary guidance, friendship, and spiritual shelter when I have needed it the most.

Appreciation for all my Douaihy, Mackinder, and Mangiola family (here and my ancestors), and for Barb Sabo. Infinite gratitude to my brilliant sister-in-law, Sienna Baskin, who reads the first and fifteen drafts of everything I write, my parents, Francine and Thomas Douaihy, and my best friend/twin sister Christa Douaihy, for your support, strength, and great humor. Thanks especially to my amazing mother for taking me to museums and encouraging an artistic practice.

This book is dedicated to Bri Hermanson—muse, collaborator, dreamer, and adventurer. Our story has just begun.

Notes

"Maidservant" was written after seeing Artemesia Gentileschi's remarkable painting *Judith Slaying Holofernes*. Many artists have explored this tale, and Gentileschi's unique interpretation, but I wanted to reimagine the inner world of the maidservant.

"Who Killed Belle Starr?" was inspired by the real, unsolved murder of Belle Starr, Oklahoma's Bandit Queen. To write the poem, I consulted narratives and family histories from the Land Run and the Pioneer Woman Museum in Ponca City, Oklahoma.

"V" was written in the legacy of Stephen Scalese—a luminous artist whom I had the great fortune to know in his brief life.

"Jasmine" was inspired by the delightfully mischievous poem "Making Tapenade" by Greg Hewitt.

I

MAIDSERVANT

I'd do anything, anything she asked.
I hoped she'd want to walk the olive grove—
with hues so green the bees were confused—
but as she crept into my tent she wept.
She had a plan: "We must slay Holofernes."
"*We*," she said.
She would trick him with wine & perfume.
I ticked down days with cuts
in her secret belt; as I dressed her
I sliced lines into thin leather.
We learned from the butcher how to hold
the ear, tilt the head, arc the blade.
We choreographed: Judith underneath me,
her will making me stronger. *Harder*,
she yelled. *Harder*. I practiced holding her down
the way I would restrain him. Sweat burned
my chin. His last night he was drunk & quiet,
hardening like lava on cold earth.
Velvet drapes let in one rod of light.
We worked fast—two fires close enough
to bleed into one. His skin tore easily
as he tangled the sheets.
I wouldn't say that I had doubts—I didn't—
but as the life in his eyes reversed,
a sudden wind choked our candle.
She followed a star & I followed her,
steady as a vow. No light save for above,
one volt between planets that will never touch.
She was named queen but sits alone
in her tent. We speak no longer of velvet,
the enemy's jaw. How I wish I could be
as pure as darkness, taking whatever it wants.

Girls Like You

It's too early to swim. You always said that,
even in August. Those summers at your lake,
drunk from one beer, we talked
until our jaws hurt. The dock's edge
wore smoother each year
by hands feeling their way out of water.

Bring smokes, lo mein, PJs. We slept
on the same porch swing, ate
from each other's forks, sketched,
passed a cigar back & forth
as your grandma scowled.
Girls like you will never get nice boys.

One twilight, the sky split quick
above your grandma's backstroke.
She said that lightning felt like getting hit
in the face with a flaming oar—
the danger of defying nature.
Thunder rippled the lake's skin.

Before the rain, you took my hand,
led me to the dock
to save our drawings.
It was quiet near the dogwood.
Invisible stones
stabbed my bare feet.

Night snuck in fast. As rain
sliced air, we ducked
under trees, stood still.
I could not see
through the changing light,
could not find a path out.

Perch

A fish convulsing in parched brown grass.
I didn't know the rules of lean & slack,
& yanked her out of the lake too hard.
Drowning in air, her slick gills glittered
like meteor shower coral. I let her
writhe, I let her die, like choosing
to fail 8th grade Bible class.
Better than letting Leviticus list my sins:
how I took the bait,
how I opened my mouth for the chum.
I was weak & terrible.
You'd think that the sound of a fish
choking on air is *only* terrible,
but like metal twisting in a collision,
there are frequencies ears rarely hear,
so they perk & notice. I think
of the perch as you breathe under water
in the bathtub. I'm lying
in the first grass after the thaw.
Will I ever learn how to give & take
in a way that might save us both?

Past Lives

On the new map, Pennsylvania is long as the wagon
our husbands ride. Our houses bookend the block,
so we pass each other most afternoons.
When gypsies rolled in, you wanted
your tarot read, but they hypnotized
and robbed you. Purse, hats, rings—
gone. Even your lovebird, Pretty.
They slithered through your side door
like secrets slipped, a red skirt tore
on the pear tree. I broke your trance
with a kiss, something small,
you won't remember.
Pretty flies back the Tuesday next.

***

Geishas in far corners of Gion.
We pin our hair, paint our necks,
write love poems on plum blossoms
to sail down the pond's throat.
We pass each other most afternoons,
your perfume a curtain in the corridor.
At night I lie awake—the wet roof
beaten by wet wind.

***

We pass each other most afternoons
but share the same Physics class.
Our room is full of charts & maps—
the cosmos bleeds like a watercolor bird.
Without raising your hand you say every star
is a sun, & we share the same chemistry.
Light travels millions of years, just to be seen.
How long would you wait?
How far would you go?

Kimono

Junior year raced by with each gym class
we ditched. We took buses just to see
where they'd go, threw bottles from
Kate's roof to hear how things break.

One night, she stopped her car
& ran toward the woods, singing.
What if there were some guy, I whined,
some dude with a knife?
She looped her arm through mine,
it'll make a good story.
The forest's dark center hummed,
tugged deep, in my molars,
but we stood at the tree-line,
too scared to walk in.
At Denny's (only place open)
for pancakes (only thing they did right),
the waitress smirked with her whole head
as she led us to our two-top.
We shared a Newport, discussed logistics
of third base. *That waitress . . . what a dyke,*
Kate glared as she fed me from her plate.
Gross, I said.
With each eyelash I wished
the stained folds of the ripped booth
could keep us lost there, lost, like fallen coins.
Ten years later, getting high in her bedroom

              the day before her wedding.
Who gets married in a kimono? I ask,
pointing the closet, ajar,
to her dress—fold under fold,
like the code of cadence inside words.
Makes a good story, she says.
In the mirror, clouds mock
like smoke, seen but never held.
Then she lifts her knee
to show me her lace garter.
It's so soft, I forget it's on.
Here, feel.

Four Ways to View a Fist of Clay

I. From the Right

Red dye. Dying firefly
in her cupped hands.
Stop shaking—shaping.

II. From the Left

Its cold weight numbs her.
Fingerprints make dragons
whose bones become stone.

III. From Below

Bird eats moth. Mouth. Her eye
slides side to side. Do wings take
or receive flight? Alight here.

IV. From Above

The clay molds her:
sacrament of storm.
It takes, she gives, it takes.

Fog

3 a.m. In the backseat
Kate's asleep
with her head in my lap,
her gnome boyfriend
driving us home.
I shouldn't let him drive
but I'm too tired to argue.
The woods swallow light,
hold it in, like drawing
someone's breath
into your mouth.
Kate's hair is still wet
on my legs,
the gnome's pointy head
barely peeks over his seat.
Tonight Kate & I split
a case of beer
then swam to the middle
of the lake, too drunk
to reach the other side.
Walking to the car
she held my hand,
said she could never
love him, but it's better
than being alone.
      We move so fast we float.
Maybe the gnome
isn't even driving,
it's fog carrying us
through trees
like leaves
sewn into a gale.

Festival of the Hungry Ghost, Hong Kong

Dragon boats still search for her—
the Empress who drowned long ago,
when stories changed
every time they were sung.
She was pregnant.
At least her ghost is not alone.

I couldn't believe in the idea
of ghosts, even as the wind—
a press of calloused hands—
held my face like dead weight.
I spit over the ferry railing
to watch something sink.
What's wrong with you?
Belts of stars roared,
tiny fires blinked code on the shore
as women burned fake money
to placate hungry, roaming ghosts.
Small sacrifices.

In the hotel I ate so fast
I burned my tongue,
swallowed dumplings whole,
stabbed chopsticks into the wine bottle
to catch the plum—a baby's fist behind glass.
Everything looks perfect behind glass.
The bed was long & low,
no pillows, no blankets,
sheet stained from the drying line.
I bit your lip so hard it bled;
you flipped me on my stomach,
traced your thumb down my spine
like a fin tearing the skin of water,
tried to slide your whole fist inside.

At dawn I woke to someone leaving
a tray of moon cakes by the door.
Legend says rebels hid notes
in each cake to foment revolution,
but how many were lost, eaten with tea?
Can you feel it, the moment
someone's wish disappears inside?

At Saint Vincent's Hospital Watching My Girlfriend Get Her Stomach Pumped

You don't want to know how it smelled—rust & crusted scum,
like a half-eaten paw, the chewing, chewing for relief. We were 22, 23,

old enough to know better. We smoked inside back then, bought coke
on Avenue B, bartender's crack-rot teeth, apocalypse chic.

You don't want to know how it sounded, the volcano of siren, EMTs
from Queens, ambulance on the sidewalk, squeal of stretcher wheels.

In the ER, a man tripped hard, no sheet to hide the screwdriver stuck
in his wrist. The Hasidic nurse, Hester, stacked white socks in a tight pile.

We were lost, but together almost somewhere. She, a sinkhole,
& I, quicksand, happy to be taken, eaten, even by nothing.

You don't want to know how chapped her lips felt after they emptied her stomach,
so mad her shut eyes, the way undead say nothing while punching through coffins,

too hungry to be pissed, scabs growing over scabs, craters of bubbling sores.
Her breath thin as I traced her mouth with my finger: *It's okay, baby,*

like the sepia scientist as the village burns, wishing for strength
not to run, but to stay, slay the demon, the fiend we sired.

ENDINGS

Leave early, when she's half-asleep.
If she wakes, say something
about a big meeting, a late train.
Take only what fits
in your backpack.

Leave a five-page tome.
Quote Plath: *beauty is painful.*
It would get ugly if you stayed.
Keep the duvet.

Leave like a hailstorm.
A maelstrom. Overturn trees.
Shake stones from their settings.

Or, go
slow. Stop complimenting
her hair in the morning.
Stop kissing her neck
when she's washing dishes.
Stop sliding your hand
beneath the skirt
you bought at Spitalfields.
Forget to buy her favorite
linseed bread & Chardonnay.
Don't talk during dinner,
give one-word answers: *Fine.*
Tell her she looks unwell,
too skinny, so tired.
Maybe you should try vitamins.
Tell her she seems confused.
Is everything okay?
She's on the phone
with her sister.
She's crying.

Rorschach

It's a spell brewing in the witch's palm,
a storm stewing in the sorcerer's book.
It's the milky opal of the Empress's ring.
The sea as seen from Madagascar,
Madagascar as seen from space—
the ten fly-eyes of the multiverse.
It's a tide teased by the moon,
reunion of left & right,
though it must be read from the center out.
It's the hostage squinting through the keyhole,
stab of the bayonet that started the war,
whistle of someone nervous—
her voice meandering in a lie.
It's the muscle of exhale, fever high,
body memory of a tear, tear-drop,
split, split-second. It's pain in reverse,
amplitude of rain righting itself.
It's the wave of om inside a white dome,
last cut of lace before the factory closed,
loopy oooo of the last cuckoo left,
eyeball of verb inside every bird.
It's a pink organ, the insides inside us,
first peck of beak through shell.
It's me through the glass, spinning like a dervish.
If I turn fast enough I can shake out this gnawing,
the way a spin cycle drains stains from cloth.
Even when I'm still, something's clawing.
Wherever I go I bring this ink with me—
too tame to be feral, too feral for a name.

WIFE

a villanelle

A word—curious spell. Wife means your, mine.
I thought wife meant half—a has-been she.
Two lives find tune, like jasmine on one vine.

"Wife" made me cringe. It meant reduce, resign.
It was my shield from what I couldn't be.
Two lives find tune, like jasmine on one vine.

We can marry now. It's legal! It's fine!
Even then, would you know to unlock me?
Two lives find tune, like jasmine on one vine.

I was a room with no door or exit sign.
Love meant limit—logic I didn't see.
A word—curious spell. Wife means your, mine.

How steady is a house on a fault line?
I never unpacked; I could always flee.
Two lives find tune, like jasmine on one vine.

But in the first light she traces my spine,
maybe—yes, maybe—can we be a we?
A word—curious spell. Wife means your, mine.
Two lives find tune, like jasmine on one vine.

Avon

The first married woman
I ever kissed was named Lane
in Scranton's only gay bar
hidden between the jail

& Lace Factory. She was 5'9",
blond, sold Avon.
What are you drinking? I asked.
Whatever's clever, she said.

I liked her gold earrings,
diamond ring singing
against the glass of
a happy-hour gimlet.

I hung on her every word,
elbows glued to the warped
bar railing as she decoded
a sad future in my palms.

At 10 we paid the tab
& played make-over
in her car. *Try this.*
Dire-red kiss marks

smirked on the back
of my hands, like chaperones,
droning Greek chorus
before a great flood.

She showed me how
to blot & blend, stretch
shadows with the pad
of my middle finger.

If Avon made mascara that didn't run,
she said as she held open my eye,
*I'd sell it forever. But it runs, hon,
& at some point, we all cry.*

II

New York

We were on a mission to see just how alive our lives were.
Remember how we danced in back of the bar
& were asked to stop? I told the bartender
I'd trade a carton of cigarettes
if she let us keep dancing. It worked.
Remember the guy with the tattooed face
& step-dancers in matching lamé?
On Avenue C I kicked the stereo on the curb
when stereos were big enough for a shoe.
It was the night the only money you had
was a one-hundred-dollar bill.
It fell into the bodega bag with the blackberries.
I washed it & laid it out to dry.
"Now you're a money launderer," you said.
Sometime later you would hail a cab & feel
the city's anxious heart hammering the pavement.
How can you explain it? The ease of falling
up tiled stairs, our boomeranged voices
in the blue hallway, trying to catch acid rain.
That June, you hung a white sheet in your garden
for the Fellini party, wore a black wig
& called me Marcello all night.
I stirred Martinis with a pen.
The trumpet player practiced upstairs,
Fellini ghosted on repeat, &
the cat escaped through the back window
cracked so thin, my fist barely fit through.
We sat on the steps making posters of the cat,
though what was lost would never be found again.

HEART

the Komodo dragon
never knew how big it was
until it was stolen from the island
& caged behind ribs.
it talks, but no one talks back.
too ugly to watch closely.
too strange to trust alone.
how could we?
the second you fall asleep
it will escape.

Mother's Day

Quiet storm in the valley
& in the half light the bird uses
her whole body—even her startled eyes—
to claim an inch of wind.
She flies or falls—nothing in-between.
Does she live divided
because she was torn in places
she never thought would tear,
then held in a bowl of strange hands?
Years ago you held my weak neck.
It's the curve of the spine
that helps a baby escape
the mother, but it breaks, easy,
the way a voice snaps in a lie,
collapses inside itself.
I laid naked today on smooth wood
in the searing sauna,
fingering a hard knot
at the base of my skull.
The stranger next to me
was so close I could taste her
sweat, feel her throat constrict
as she swallowed. Later, we bathed
near each other, not talking—
listening to hot water moan,
pipes close to exploding.
Like most days, I think of how often
I fail you, too weak to chase
the brutal world away. It is impossible
to list every promise I've broken,
instead I cry into my hands.
I'm disgusting when I cry,
though the symmetry of tears
pooling in my life-lines is almost pretty.
They could be your palms, you know?
I look so much like you. Strange
how only the unknowable is worth knowing,
the hand pulling away is the only hand
worth hanging on to.

First Time

I didn't know what to do.
Neither did you.

The hotel room itched
with clocks,

wall to wall,
tocks ticking.

We sat on the edge
of the bed,

I opened your hand,
tried to read

your palm, locked
code, engraved stone.

I went first.
Your lips so cold.

You didn't blink,
looked so serious

like you wanted
to cry.

VENICE

For an eternal resting place,
the Basilica is bloody loud.
Saints must be heavy sleepers.
The Ranieri brothers didn't use
blueprints to build it,
just a frame of sea & sky.
The Doge blinded them
so they'd never repeat
their masterpiece. Beauty
is dangerous to hold.

No cars, riddle of roads.
Vendors on boats sell lemons, cherries,
olive oil soap sliced into bricks,
white fruit with pink flesh.
In a silver dish: hazelnuts, broken
& whole as a dropped string of pearls.

A maze at its heart, stairs all the same
under bare bulbs. But I could get lost
anywhere. Sometimes I close my eyes,
feel my way out of strange rooms.
It's okay if we're lost, you say,
shifting your purse from hand to hand.
I'm tired of standing
on verandas too small for us
just to brush arms.
You point to the sea.
Do you see?
I see.
Soft green water
climbing marble stairs,
steps leading nowhere.

How to View a Solar Eclipse

Find two pieces of cardboard.
One is the screen.
One, a pinhole camera.

Pierce a pinhole in one piece
with a pen. Ask your girlfriend
to help. If she's out,
take a pen from her desk.

Rest the screen against a tree,
hold your pinhole camera high,
back to the eclipsing sun.
Don't wonder where
your girlfriend's been all week
or read her email
when looking for the pen.

Sunlight passes through the hole
forming a projection.
Recall your first kiss in the woods,
spell rippling through your veins,
both of you hovering. Don't think
about how long it's been
since you've made out.

Focus on the hole; imagine
fitting inside, crawling
through a tiny damp tunnel.
How long can you hold your breath?
How much smaller
can you get?

Globe

When I was a kid I needed
to hear doors close
behind me.
I was bored by board games.
Puzzles meant migraines.
The impossible ships
moored in glass bottles
couldn't anchor me.
I was never hot for playing house.
What I craved was the old globe,
its floating gold tilt.
I spent hours with it
in the dim den, staring,
hoping to absorb the orb in each eye
the way a spookfish uses mirrors
to see through ink.
I spun it, tracing countries,
seas I couldn't pronounce.
One summer, I walked away.
I was eight. It was Jersey,
and the pull of the shore—
the voice of somewhere—
was so strong I couldn't hear
my parents screaming my name.
The louder they yelled
the less I heard. How could I know
my need to leave would never
leave me? 12 zip codes
in 10 years. Maybe some wheat
is too scabbed, too sick
for threshing.
Now, in our wood home,
so rooted & calm,
I plug coordinates
into Google Earth—
my new, flat globe—
but the closer I zoom
the more the image blurs.

Too Late

a triolet

I burned the last wood you found.
    We chose to till where nothing could grow,
    like the river paved to build downtown.
I burned the last wood you found
    as the moon rises without a gown.
    Was our stream a stream, or melting snow?
I burned the last wood you found.
    We chose to till where nothing could grow.

Ten-Word Love Stories

In Hong Kong we ate moon cakes by a window.

***

You rolled your own cigarette, then exhaled through your nose.

***

I noticed no ring on your finger. Or did I?

***

Your red dress hung tight & low as a comma.

***

Not sure what else to get. How's the lotus root?

***

I ordered hot congee so you'd miss the last ferry.

***

The taxi was quiet. I whispered, *Here is fine. Thanks.*

***

The shade behind the bed let in just enough light.

***

Your eyes were horizon blue—the first breath above water.

***

Dawn. I woke alone, on the veranda, under windchimes.

END OF THE HOLIDAY

The radio says frost: new cold front's on the way.
But more ice won't fit; the earth can't take it.

The ground is brittle as a letter
slipped into a spell book & forgotten.

Christmas was yesterday; dishes collapse
in the sink, coffee crusts the carafe.

Dad's at the mall, exchanging sweater sizes.
Mom's at work, with the boss dad despises.

Wind woke me last night, rattled the roof
shook grandma's chimes loose.

My old room chokes with dust, old porn, torn
skirt, gold heels I wore once, to the prom.

Mom won't let me clean, won't throw anything out.
Except the Madonna posters. *You never needed those.*

On the porch, dogs growl, noses twitching,
like they smell a stranger in the shrub, hiding.

I'd stay the week, but the morning bus
goes straight to New York. No stops.

Rock

How foolish
we were to make
promises when we
are designed to break
apart, to find our simplest
form, to return to the thinnest
vibrating string. We begin as one
then the cord is cut. All we are are clues,
molecules glued, atoms aching to be small,
smaller, smallest. All the decades, all the pages
of calendars ripped & forgotten. Each day distills into
one moment, one night, one hour, fragile as the path through
oak. One beer, one cigarette, both of us shivering. You put your
cold hand under my shirt. One rock smooth enough to sit. We both fit.

SCARLET FEVER

Born four weeks early—more bird than baby—your parents
watched you sleep, tiny red chest rising, falling.

When you got scarlet fever no one knew what to do.
You didn't cry, just burned sleepless, even in an ice bath.

Thirty years later you're still one degree hotter,
vein to vein small flames creep, limb to limb.

Our first night together the bed floated,
heat flooded the bedroom, a bath overflowing.

The hands of fire reached through your own hands,
pulled my face to your heart—a tropical bird in flight.

Since you left, it's me who can't sleep, can't cry.
Tried to eat once but turned on the wrong burner, high.

A glass dish exploded, scratched the walls, cut my hands,
like a kid climbing a tree, too excited to feel the tearing.

Limb to limb, higher, sweating, higher,
deeper, higher, tearing, unable to stop.

Envy

We envy the sea—
me and rain. Nothing falls deep
just to rise again.

III

I Said the Bruises Were From Dancing

because it's hard to explain that I shattered my knee

& sprained my wrist falling from the shopping cart we needed

to surf while rolling on Ecstasy at 4 a.m. Never was a mission

more clear. For years we dreamed of surfing that Price Chopper

near the Lace Factory where a Coke, chips, & soup cost $2.50.

Dancing was the best excuse, for we did dance then: sweaty raves

in empty barns on nights so clear we felt constellations pulse.

As I careened into the curb, two wheels broke. *Fuck me!*

Kate laughed as I picked gravel out of my knee-cap,

sat so close her heat screamed through my jean jacket.

I wanted her to think I was tough—crazy enough to try anything.

How often I wanted to put my mouth around the words.

I've lost count of the times I almost mailed an envelope

of cash to pay for that cart—

all of the groceries it should have transported,

all of the baby legs that could have kicked out of the basket seat,

all of the dreamers & surfers robbed of their chance.

But that Price Chopper closed ten years ago.

CONFESSION

I loved kissing you
through the shower curtain.
You looked beautiful &
dead, like Laura Palmer
when the fisherman found her—
naked, wet, wrapped in plastic.
Your eyes slippery, see-through
as scales, your lips, purple.
It's sick, I know,
but not as bad as the fact
that we'll never shower
together again.

Plum

No. Don't forgive me.
I ate your plum
that was in the icebox
that you were probably
saving
since Sunday. Don't say,
Oh, no worries,
as you hang up your coat.
I ate your fucking plum.
Don't forgive me, like always,
even when I forget to set
the alarm, or shower
for twenty minutes
though the film starts in ten
& it's a hike in the hail.
Surely when I flirt
with the bartender, come
home five hours late
with my shirt inside out
you shouldn't forgive me.
So this delicious plum,
so sweet & so cold
is the end, because you are
probably starving
this time of night
& that was
the last plum
ever to exist;
you'll be plagued by pangs
of hunger for the phantom plum.
When you start buying
only plum-colored clothes,
filling every crossword
with P-L-U-M,
I will send you to safety—
far from fruit-bearing crops of any kind,
to the Plum Rehabilitation Institution
in Scranton,
where you will age
into plum-free eternity,
for which, of course,
you will forgive me.

Reality Show

The Real House Cats of Beverly Hills

You've *never* seen cat fights like this. Prrrfect is your best ally,
unless you're sitting in her sunbeam. Beware: this kitten has class—
& claws. These felines enjoy their fine nine lives:
cat nip labyrinths, Louis Vuitton scratching posts,
beluga caviar on silver spoons. Outrageous? Perhaps.
But don't we all share the need to knead—to be held,
comforted? Spoiler alert: a single ball of yarn
could unravel it all.

•••

Dancing On the Stars

Gravity meets *Fame!* in this stellar series.
Twelve astronauts pair with professional dancers
to learn tap & jazz. Will these high steppers
land the Salsa on Saturn, Lindy Hop
on the lunar surface, Merengue on Mars?
How free can you be when there's no fear of falling?
Tune in Sunday for a show that's out of this world.

•••

The Real World: Downton Abbey

This is the true story of seven strangers picked to live in a castle—
a handsome castle—a soaring sight of Jacobethan might,
faced in ancient stone. Some live upstairs, some downstairs.
After too much mead, two maids kiss in the broom closet.
Disgusting, growls Mister Puck. Spurned by his love interest
he grabs his pipe, slams an elfin door, & menaces like a gargoyle
in the hedgerow. Twelve hours of chimney sweeping tucker them out;
they sleep deeper, harder than at home. In sepia dreams
images flicker: love letters intercepted, tiny spoons, bells dance
on the wall like foxglove in strong wind, trousers creased so sharp
they could de-finger. The waft of ghost bread confuses the cast
as they toss & turn on stiff beds. In the walls, mice marvel at their snoring.
4am—wake up—soundtrack of the black iron stove. Wood on fire—
pop, pop, pop—like the joints of a broken body descending stairs.

Neither

if what hovers has a color   it is the taste of a mirror
                                  dilating pupil
                                  water breathing air
                                  in the eyeball's pond

if the eye is solid liquid   so is every cell
                                  each inch raw with need
                                  limbs try to escape
                                  in plain sight
                                  like rain

if rain has a voice   she doesn't use it
                                  won't tell you more
                                  than she already has
                                  maybe she sounds like no sound at all
                                  just the contraction
                                  expansion of breath

if breath is the beginning   it is the dream you love
                                  but can't remember why
                                  fragile as the tree-seam
                                  where beetles hide
                                  yes beetles play dead
                                  but the hawk always finds them

if death is the end   we live in-between
                                  neither/neither
                                  yes i know the word
                                  but can't pronounce it
                                  un/familiar as staring
                                  into my own eyes
                                  in the pond's warped mirror
                                  my reflection hovering
                                  not like a question,
                                  but a demand,
                                  ransom

Text Me

1
No the train now.
I would ruby if I could.
I want to vouch your face.
In in loud with you.
I loud you.

2
On the train now
I would stay if I could.
I want to touch your face.
I'm in love with you.
I love you.

Survival Instinct

Saturn chews his children headfirst
before they can overthrow him,
their vein-thin arms
raised like halleluiah.

Medea sends her sons to deliver
poisoned clothes to her husband's lover.
Jason, she calls, falsetto. The plan works;
the dress eats skin, ignites tiny bites.

In the woods a cat will kill
the newborn too small to survive.
Teeth to scruff, a quick shake,
the kitten's neck breaks like a voice.

What makes it so mad—
the horror,
the shame,
or that you understand?

How We Do It

This is how we do it: Drink forty espressos, light the fuse, & dive in screaming.

This is how we do it: Piece by piece—de-bead a skillion beads of sequence
to find which one swallowed the sun.

This is how we do it: Shine it & brine it & serve it with wine.

This is how we do it: One. Two. Do over.

This is how we do it: The telephone game. You go then I go then you go then I go.
What was done will be undone so the end is only new.

This is how we do it: Actually, we don't. It's done. The opera's been sung.
Energy is neither created nor destroyed—just transferred. One breath out, one in.

Start

Start at the end
with the heroine victorious,
her foe defrocked,
nailing his shutters shut.
Start aloft, the bird in flight.
Reverse engineer the journey
of what becomes itself
when it's alone.

Start in the middle.
On ice. Let the story flip
itself to death
like a fish plucked
from a hole in the ice.
Start inside vermilion,
inside the insides of the rabid bear
ripping fish flesh
for her sleuth of blind cubs.

Start at the beginning.
A false spring
that lures lilacs to pop.
Build no plot
so no ending emerges—
just chance, potential,
fascia laced over bone,
knee caps ready to run.
A window open to the rain.

Tiny Sun

I always hide behind my hair, even when I don't have hair.
I disappeared inside my shaved head, identity *de facto* of college, coming out.
Camouflaged in plain sight, a faux reveal, ersatz openness of skin & neck.
But the locks grew back, as confused as I was. I keep inventing new ways
to duck: my long hair & manicure, kitten heels & denim skirts.
At the Cherry Tavern, a frat boy barked when I refused his drink:
"But you don't *look* gay." Describing me to a new friend, my mom called me
a lollipop lesbian. "Sorry, I meant lipstick!" What if there were infinite ways
to be at ease—each one surprising? Thirty spokes join together, but it is the
empty center that allows the wheel to roll. What is Earth but a rock spinning on ice?
Gravity's just a high-wire walk. To X-ray joy reveals a tug-of-war between crying
& laughing, because all things end. Look at the delicate skin of the quarterback,
his thin fingers as he passes. How lithe is the woman with her blond hair,
holding a hammer like she invented it. Don't we all inherit hot & cold, January
& June, a comet & moon? Even now as it roars the rain holds light—so bright—
as if a tiny sun burned in each drop.

Oracle

I touch it as he talks—
my jaw—
it's small, like the bell
of a tulip or fig, rotting
at the base of a tree.
He's like the rest
who come to Delphi
from Parnassus, Thrace,
Corinth & Cyprus,
the darker their skin
the longer their journey.
They don't see me inside
this column of vapor,
they don't care what I look like,
they want only my voice.
My mouth is a cave
behind a waterfall,
invisible, except
when they need hiding.
They want to win battles,
stretch empires,
mend the ship's weak hull.
Men need war, men I want
to unfold like maps
on cold marble.
Bring almonds, figs,
bring red wine in clay bowls.
Agamemnon said he closed his eyes
as he pulled a blade
deep from the meat of his thigh.
Veins in his temple
harden into spiny thistle.
Bay leaves burn near his bare feet.
I'm tired of talking. I'm done.
I want to be quiet as mud,
a village razed.
One day, a map I help you craft
will destroy me,
the way lines on a face
trace years of laughter
and also predict death.

IV

Reminder

Please power down all electronics during the performance.

Please refrain from taking flash-photography.

Please remove any blinking devices or flashing lights of any kind.

Please extract all flashes of brillliance or flashy memories, like the time
you got decked out in the red dress & wore the heels to meet a woman
whose face has since been erased from every flash drive, hard-drive, & cloud.

Please crawl inside the photograph of that night & delete yourself.

Please blink your eyes enough times to delete every image you want to forget,
like a camera in reverse.

Please wake up one hundred years ago, in the pastel room of the first flash photo.
Note the black brimmed hats, garments stitched by real hands, the rectitude
with which the parents sit. Assume that the pixie children seated in the front
with their sulking shoulders & petulant expressions would rather be singing,
running barefoot in the sun & grass. Next to the photographer under his thick cloak
the first-ever flash lamp explodes like a scream of someone surprised. Hear how
the world sighed, for now we could see in the dark, though we were never meant to.
Notice how long the sting of flash stays in your eyes, etching images behind your lids.
Let the chemicals burn your nose as tears roll, for what happens only once should happen
only once.

Who Killed Belle Starr?

The Tracks
Just as train tracks live in the most curious of tandem, Belle Starr's tale & our tale run real close yet real far. Even as they crest & wind, never will two rails meet.

The House
We all know why a bandit is what a bandit is. Belle Starr—a female bandit, about as rare a happenin' as a fur coat in August—is no exception.

The Courthouse
Myra Maybelle Reeves Reed Starr—The Fugitive Known As Belle Starr—Was Born In Carthage, Missouri, In The Year 1848. Despite Decent Bringing-Up, In Which The Fugitive Received Proper Education & Became A Pianist Of Some Regard, Belle Starr Took To The Crime-Life Faster Than A Vole Takes To Munching On Beans. After The Lawless Degenerate Jim Reed—Belle's First Of Three Husbands—Shot A Man, He & Belle Went On The Lam: Robbing Banks, Bribing, Rustling Horses, Thieving Cows, & Quite Regular Counterfeiting, Most Convincing.

The Hutch
Shot at a wolf that snuck like a hex into the bunny hutch. Belle Starr is guilty of many a crime, but she could smite a wolf from any distance, & in that sense, she is notable.

The Beginning
We all know how it started: Jesse James's gang hid at her farm when she was a baby—small enough to crawl in a boot. Belle was but a tiny thing when she got a taste of the outlaw way. After the War claimed her family's Inn & the life of her brother Bud—who could not carry a tune even in a bucket, but nonetheless was beloved by Belle—she turned crime-dizzy. We tried, but there is no sense-talking after a new leather saddle & twirl of purple velvet capture you.

The Wanted Poster
Belle Starr Sighting: 5th Of August. Stay Vigilant. Keep Hands On Weapons In Presence Of Fugitive. Look Out For The Plumed Hat & Whirl Of Purple Velvet Skirt That Signify Starr. Do Not Look Into The Convict's Obsidian Eyes, For Even The Prison Matron Was Charmed By Belle. Do Not Trust. Call Local Bounty For Reprimand.

The Hoof Prints
Hard heat. Hot as the hinges of Hell. Baby sick with dizzy. We are not sleeping. John is working for Mr Adams, haying for six days. I work for R Green, sewing brooms. I sell a broom or two of my own, on the side like. But do not tell R Green, for I feel a bit of an outlaw myself. My suspicions grow that Belle is riding here in the trance of night. Hoof tracks design the dirt in a pattern not unlike Belle's plumed hat with the broadest of brim.

The Paper
Hoed some. Walked to town to buy the Paper which reported no exploits of Belle Starr.

The Horse
Sister told me that Mr Reeves told her that he caught sight of Belle Starr & her third husband—the Creek Indian, Jim July. Jim July is fifteen years Belle's junior. Well we were right shocked with this nugget of fact, but a strange sense of pride accompanied our scorn. Sister said that Mr Reeves said that the two rode on horseback so fast it was as if the hooves did not touch ground. Sister suggested a possession by the D-vil Himself. We suspect more accurately that, although we disagree with her dishonest ways, Belle's riding skills are quite unmatched. In my sleeplessness I keep one ear perked-or the sound of silent horseplay.

The Hoe
Hoed some. Broke the hoe. Went to T Trout & got new hoe. All forenoon Baby cried. Sick with the dizzy again. To kill a squirrel I imagined Belle Starr's gun resting on her shoulder which had the immediate effect of steadying me. Mercury at 93.

The House
Pleasant day of sewing brooms. Forenoon Mercury hit 95. Hotter than a billy goat in a pepper patch. Went to sell a broom to T Trout whose hogs are dropping off with some new disease. Lost a dozen head in two weeks. Mr Reeves said that because Belle has emptied one too many banks with no disguise upon her face, most likely she would be shot in the back. Though she criminalizes, I would rather Belle not get shot in the back. Sister held a quilting. We, Mother, & D (that newcomer), helped quilt. In-corporating a purple tile on the quilt was my idea.

The Vole
Walked to Owasso & back. Mother watched Baby who is still sick. It is ten miles there, ten miles back. Traded butter for clover. Used the hoe to kill the vole. At night we washed. John threshed for Mr Powell. We asked Mr Powell if he had heard of new exploits of Belle Starr & her youngen, Jim July. Nope, he replied, with a side eye of bemusement.

The Courthouse
It Is Declared That Belle Starr's Death In 1889 In Briartown, Oklahoma, Was Either An Accidental Shooting Or Death By Murder. The Coroner Is Conclusive In His Conclusion. Belle Starr Was Shot Off Of Her Favorite Horse In Her Purple Skirt With Her Own Double-Barrel Rifle. While Most Folk Nodded Agreeably Upon News Of Belle Starr's Death, Select Others Believed A Back-Shot Ambush To Be Disrespectful Of The Deceased.

The House
Windy to-day. Mended a shoe & sewed a broom. Baby still sick with dizzy. The Paper

prints few details about Belle Starr's death. It remains unsolved, a mystery as peculiar as the sinister spin of a tornado. But, if you ask me, most surely the killer is Belle's covetous neighbor. In the undesirable occurrence you must shake hands with him before buying corn, you will no doubt feel that his fingers are still hot with shot. As disagreeable it might be to thieve, it is tough-goin' out here, most definite for a lady. Belle Starr (a competent pianist from what the Paper reported) seemed destined for different livin'. For certain she had addictions: to fleein' & finery, purple velvet skirts & hats with the broadest of brim. What woman has coin enough for such wares? You know the sayin': no lard unless you boil the hog.

Wax

What would it sound like
if we said what we felt
the second we sensed it?
What if we never edited,
revised?

What if there were
no such thing as nothing?
Would it surprise you?

What if gravity could push
continents back together?
What if we didn't need a map
to find the way back?
If we asked for help
& let ourselves cry,
would we realize:
no one knows?

What if the storm came again
& there were no reason to be
anywhere except here,
at this wood table?
Your hair in your eyes.
This bowl of figs & torn bread.
This candle that will melt
into a lake of wax
& never reset.

GIMMIE A BREAK

The photo on the fridge speaks to Nell, as she pours coffee,
during sunrise. *Nell*, the photo says, its voice, familiar.
Dad? she asks. *Yeah, it's me.*
The photo shows a father & daughter kneeling
on a blanket in a park back East. They hadn't spoken
since their last fight, the night before he died.
You ran away, he said from his high bed.
You could have been the next Mahalia Jackson,
but threw it away. Why? To sing in nightclubs.
She bites her lip hard enough to bleed. *Gimme a break*, she says,
holds the image, traces anything that still holds light:
a blossom, about to fall from the branch;
a bubble from a little girl in a stroller; her sleepless eyes
drowning in gray circles, like seeds that want to fruit, but can't.
She thinks of her dad, cherry tobacco like cheap musk
on his hands after shoveling snow, the family fussing
about her church songs, though her dreams
unfurled red drapes, spotlights, smoke.
Can't God hear me anywhere? she cried after she ran away.
The hot coffee brings her back to the cold chrome table.
Relax, she tells herself. But can we ever be still?
Blood can only be restless in veins.
Some days, when she is hollow, when Chief
tells her to sew & sweep, she worries she'll never be whole,
but a deep breath into her secret lung delivers quiet.
Time for school, & the kids file into the kitchen
with the subtle wobble of something still growing.
She covers her photo with magnets as they croon, *Nell!*
on tiptoes for cereal bowls, *Nell!* She recites it with them—
Nell—the way you state a name during a handshake
to memorize a face, someone at the market
she might like to see again, a woman she's finally ready
to know.

V

    In the park, an old woman is knitting,
talking to someone only she can see. Overhead,
a V of geese—proof of what think together & alone.
This is New York City, where neither ghosts nor geese
nor people can afford rent, so we all share holes in stone.

    Late for work, a young woman runs through the park
& sees the old woman knitting. Overheard, the V of geese
trade bird words—our language before. The young woman
leans into the fence to catch her breath: her heart claws
her rib cage, storms itch her skin. What is it, she wonders,
that keeps birds from falling, all of us from sliding into space?

    A man walks to the subway, past the park.
He notices a V of geese glowing overhead, a young woman catching
her breath against the fence, an old woman knitting with ghosts,
& remembers a lake he found during a hike. It was too cold to swim,
but he wanted to be held by something bigger & smaller
than himself. Above him, birds, proof of what appear
& disappear. He realizes how fast voices can vanish,
how silence so quickly devours song.
Before he descends, he watches the V break & re-glue.
One second late, he misses his train: the glowing tail light slips
into darkness, like an eel sucked into a hungry black beak.

Tag

I was taking selfies before they were selfies.
Self-portraits?
No, selfies.
So self-portraits.
You are, like, so literal.
Not really.
Really.
Can I take a picture of you?
Don't tag me.
I wasn't going to post it.
Then why take it?
I want to take it.
Just don't tag me.
Remember when tag was something different?
No.
It was a game.
Okay.
You know, when I tag you & you're it.
"It?"
Tag! You're it.
Okay.
You're not running.
Do I have to?
Yeah, you're it.
Why is this fun?
The chase. To be chased.
That's cute.
What's cute?
You.
I love you.
I love you.
Let's take a picture of us.
Don't tag me.

SHORE

It's a beautiful beach—white sand, windless, empty.
Nowhere to be, no hours to win or lose. Nobody
to talk to. Just you & sun in a neon hum.
Your neck is warm; skin breathes like a third lung.
In the corner of your eye you notice a shape
in the surf. Driftwood? Wreckage?
Creature who lost its way?
It floats in & out with the tide.
You can't look away.
Tentacles of some sort, twisted tangle.
Closer you walk. Closer, &
you realize it's you in the water—
a you that you haven't seen in a while.
Your eyes are closed,
eyelids stitched in mythic sleep,
skin smooth from tumbling
in the gut of the sea.
You don't know what to do.
There's no one to ask.
You kneel, but can't look too closely.
Sun drums down as you start
to pick you up, limbs slick & heavy
with the weight of years between you.
You contort like a turtle
trying to peck out of its eggshell
despite gulls casing the dune.
Finally you walk, pressing one you into the other.
You carry yourself like this, old into new, forever,
the way waves—even as they shoal & break—
feed one reach, one push to the shore.

Fourteen Ways

I have something important to tell you.
I have to tell you something important.
Have I something important to tell you?
Have I something important to tell you!
"I tell something important." You have to.
I, important, have to tell you something.
You have to something important? I tell!
Have something important to you? Tell I.
Important! I tell you something! To have!
I have (to tell you) something important.
I have to tell . . . something. You . . . important . . .
Important to I: have to tell you something.
I have something to tell you—important.
Something important to tell: I have you.

I Want to Be your Jukebox

Fonz, you don't see me that way, but when you ride tonight,
let me come. I'll hold you tight. The open road will be our
>night school.

If I were a motorcycle, I'd wreck myself & wake up
in your body shop. You'd slide under me, face greased like
>warrior paint.

Tell me: did you flunk math? If you don't care that I can't dance,
I won't mind that you can't add. No word, no number will
>divide us.

If passion is suffering, Fonz, music is torment. *The Pony* is anguish.
I'm broken; only you can turn me on. Fancy-fix me there—yes—
>right there.

When Chachi burned down Arnold's, you cried so loud coke bottles
broke. Like sin before forgiveness, like shin splints, your screams
>slice sinew.

When the parlor ignited, I didn't run. I stayed, prayed
for you at our booth, saved your crust under purple ash,
>flames raining.

Okay, okay, Fonz; it's true. I helped set the parlor alight,
but feel how fire burns clear, to purify earth, to clean,
>to heal.

V

WHO'S THE BOSS?

All journeys start by leaving, that's what Tony must have said to Sam,
packing the van, closing the door, the way epics begin.

Don't look back. In stations of the cross, you move on.
It's time to go, he smiles, pulls the key from his ripped jeans,

muscle line in his hard arms, like a sea wall
meeting sand on a Brooklyn beach

too polluted to swim. *There's an open road & a road that's hidden,
brand new life around the bend.* A theme song's being sung, just for them.

He's not sure who sings it, but he knows a thing or two:
boxing, cooking, secret blend of wind & lip to whistle. He'll teach

how to dance—steps only old folks know. She'll need to learn
how to speak Connecticut, keep friends, shake off headaches after crying.

He'll vacuum curtains upright, iron a sandwich for uptight Angeler.
Strange how it makes him feel like a man. Isn't every departure

a return to who we want to be? He'd never admit
he is scared, he doesn't even know what to call it.

All that matters: they're together in their beat-up van, hands taking flight
out the windows, future as *go* as the green light ahead.

THELMA & LOUISE, DELETED SCENE

They've escaped?
Again?
Policemen hang their heads.
The sheriff with the soft spot
for red heads slips his gun
back in its holster.
They keep vanishing into thin air,
he says, *but we'll find em.*
We'll git 'em.

Miles away Thelma & Louise
glide through red dust.
The canyon is a fractal
of hidden passages
& pathways, but they feel safer
when they're lost. Louise mumbles
what could be words, stops the car,
her eyes as alive as the back roads
they've discovered, made their own.
Louise puts her hands on Thelma's face,
kisses her forehead, both eyebrows,
then her dusty lips.

Wind drills up through sand
like the phantom tides
that carved the desert,
into their knee-high cowboy boots
that, even in late '80s fuchsia,
are surprisingly chic.
They kiss for hours as red walls erode.
Memories fade: the microwave
dinners, stale beer,
bruises that will never heal.

What they've given up
was easy to lose.
They're free for the first time
& for the first time
the words come easy:
whiskey,
kiss me,
let's fly.

Don't Worry

      but I haven't been sleeping.
Night or day? Not sure. Not as cold
as you'd think, but thanks for the coat.
Must have been a fortune
to send. Can see everything
from up here, nothing is big.
Each color pulses
against the dark like sparks
when you see pain.
It doesn't rain except falling stars.
Why do we love what dies in fire?
I miss us: tango in the kitchen,
that freckle on your chin.
What are you doing
now? Can you see me?
I'm in the mouth
of the moon. Look up. I'm finally
part of something whole.
Look. We're whole.

Gold

"All that glisters is not gold."
—William Shakespeare, *The Merchant of Venice*

Or. All that glitters is gold, because gold is glitter &
glitter means flicker & flicker lives in the ing between all things.

Gold is the smell of sky changing, tall hall where erased drawings hide,
the stride of a bird with glittering wings.

Gold is the glitter-glass of a window opening,
words electrifying your body as you pray.

Gold is the glitter-guts of pirate treasure
buried in a sinking cove on a leap-year day.

Gold is the glitter-tongue flame of a fresh wood match;
watch how it eats air when it's lit.

Gold is the glitter of my lover's hair, the rotation of wrist
that makes a puzzle piece fit.

Jasmine

Gardening sucks.
All the bugs & slugs,

all that crawling & digging
on your knees, sweating.

Just when you're ready to quit
you smell it—the white perfume

of the jasmine vine. She's here,
the woman who tied garlands

of blossoms around your neck
on the ship's gangway.

Chennai air so hot your tears boil.
She is no one you know.

With your buzz cut & flat chest
she mistook you for a boy.

In the quick flash of bowing
you see fine muscles in her long throat.

Jasmine, jasmine, jasmine
in dusty, dim-lit markets,

Pondicherry, chili farms, ashrams,
women sweat, dig under the loam,

carry baskets of flowers to sell.
Slowly petals rain, slowly,

as they walk, saris & silk,
steaming rivers of pink & gold.

You bow, taking whatever she gives.
Her lips accidentally brush your forehead,

your third eye cries
like a pulse.

Water

My days are *all* water, not that 70%-of-the-human-body lie they tell us. Water is the tonic in every atom of sky & earth. The sun? It's actually water: orange floating in a vast black sea, charging the dark like electric eels tied at the tails. We're born liquid—drooling & pooling, dimpled elbows & knees—water sliding us from one world to the next. In the morning I am an envelope licked & sealed shut until I pour water down my throat with my eyes closed. Like bone, water remembers, though I will never recall in what lakes I've hid my reflection or what tears have carved my face. Ocean keeps no record of where we've sailed, but it sank Atlas in one wet second. Water shocks: an ice-bath keeps greens green after steaming—holds hues in. At night, we swallow each other—two streams sweat into one. In the same hour, nameless men are water-boarding someone in a nameless building on a nameless street. Hear that? She's in the bar bathroom splashing cold water on her face before driving home. The bartender is as uninterested as fog. Water gives, water takes. Frost likes to bite. Ice is quite delighted to burn & dismember. Water hides, water saves. Water loves to tell stories, even in death—like Ötzi the Iceman who emerged as 6,000-year-old snow melted in his narrow valley. Ice peeled back, revealing his murder, his crawl to the gnarled tree, his coat of woven bark. Ötzi's shoes of sewn grass & animal skins let him cross ice & snow, a slow-motion loner. How holy must one be to walk on water? How lonely & free? Maybe God is water; the same water that breathed eons ago lives still—in this glass held by these fingers. In the shower I remembered one line from my dream poem—one single, perfect line. As each drop of water opened each cell like an egg, the line was clear. The moment the water stopped, I forgot.

Shorts

Don't apologize. Don't preface. You're not
the only shy one—the moon's full
then undresses then wishes she wore the black top instead.
So what if you turn up to the party in shorts
after hitching a ride from Uncle Sy, when the others
don tuxes & park Jags on the shady side
of the pool. The others lean against a piano
criticizing a critically acclaimed something
as you camouflage into a caterer,
lift the Jameson, & slip out the back door.
Admit it: You'd rather pool hop than talk shop.
You are talented . . . in the art of keying cars.
Pull up your hood, use your finger
as a gun & steal your own wallet.
Eat lying down then clog the sink with your thick syrup.
Drink the Mickey, get sick & dream a fever-dream
spiraled as a fiddlehead that gets eaten by a moose
then shot by a teenager & thrown into a pickup
bound for Who Knows Where, at least the sun is shining.
Tell yourself it's okay to wear shorts, eat in bed, throw up,
to touch something—to bring your face close to it,
even the black barrel of a gun, hollow as a throat.
Anything hollow can sing.
It's okay to sit alone, near the window,
and order whiskey,
with nothing to read,
and no one to read you.

My Money

My money's on the guy in last place, the runt of the litter, the bloody knee.

My money's on the missing sock, the single lego, the lock with no key.

My money's on the run-on sentence, the misplaced comma, the Fail.

My money's on the deer in headlights, the queer, One White Whale.

My money's on the introvert, the B-/C+, the barely audible.

My money's on the The—ubiquitous, unanimous, invisible.

My money's on the iffy, the jinx, the artist screaming in the park.

My money's on the blinking cursor, the negative space, the space bar.

My money's on the secret wing, the Gelfling, the girl eating alone in her car.

My money's on the sun shower, Spring snow, the healers, the confused.

My money's on the Podling, the flat tire, the spinning wheel, the bruised.

My money's on the fading tattoo, kind-hearted outlaw, the dented & darned.

My money's on Sisyphus. Sure, the hill is high & rock is heavy, but look at those arms.

GAME OVER

Sleeping Beauty on a picnic table. You played dead as your princess
leaned in. A tiny fire started. But eight-year old girls shouldn't kiss
so you got an earful—tarred (old school!) & feathered.
Is that why you buried your desire like a break-up letter?
That's a good story. Now here's mine: It was I who was dead
until you came—your lips on my neck. Breath is the thread
that knits us together. No art or word can save us. No spell.
Rain is revenge on the windowsill, but we lay still.
Still. Your fingertips unlock me, rib by rib—my first cage—
the same fingers that cut lines alive through ink & clay.
Read my secret skin, my braille, but you will never know
how often I've killed myself in sonnets, cut my wrists to go
to sleep first, to leave first. This time, I'm writing myself Awake.
Fuck *The End*; it will tell itself. In this story I kiss you. I stay.

Modern Women

Don't ask me how,
or why, but my wife
has a sword
stuck in her chest.

I first thought: *Hot.*
She's in the circus.
We're modern women,
you never know.
No, she said, *it's real.*
Been there since I could feel.
She tried to remove it,
but her lungs lost grip,
spleen slipped.
It was the center
holding her house together.
She left it in.
What would you have done?

No. It's not easy taking taxis
or riding ski lifts.
And people sure do stare.
But in every other way
we're just a normal
lesbian couple.
We like toast.
We rescue cats.
And—don't tell her
I told you—sex is incredible.
I ride her hard,
though one inch
to the left or right
would be fatal.

Believe it or not, I still
stare. When she catches me
she smiles so crazy,
like she's high-
wire walking.
I doubt I could
catch her
if she fell.
But I'll try.

A Note on the Poet

Margot Douaihy hails from Scranton, Pennsylvania, where her love of sylvan storytelling began. She received a Master of Art degree in Creative & Life Writing from Goldsmiths, University of London, and her Bachelor of Art degree in English Writing from the University of Pittsburgh. Margot is pursing a PhD with Lancaster University and is the Editorial Director of NewBay Media's *AV Technology* magazine. She has been a writer-in-residence with the Ora Lerman Trust, Noepe Center for Literary Arts, and Montana Arts Refuge. She is a Poetry Board Member of *Philadelphia Stories* and was awarded the 2014 Karen Blomain Memorial Scholarship for literary excellence by the F. Lammot Belin Arts Foundation. In 2013, her chapbook, *I Would Ruby If I Could*, was published by Factory Hollow Press and featured in the 21st Annual Poets House Showcase in New York. Her writing has been anthologized internationally and featured in *The Sow's Ear Review*, *The Madison Review*, *Pittsburgh Post-Gazette*, *The Common*, *The Moth Magazine*, *Big Bridge*, *Belle Rêve Literary Journal*, *The Catamaran Literary Reader*, *Ducts*, and *The New Guard Literary Review*. In addition to writing and editing, Margot teaches literature, yoga, and qigong. She resides with her family in Northampton, Massachusetts.

www.ingramcontent.com/pod-product-compliance
Lightning Source LLC
Chambersburg PA
CBHW070545170426
43200CB00011B/2567